Life Changing Magic

The power of personalised
Vipassana Affirmations

Michael Kewley
Dhammachariya Paññadipa

All rights reserved.
Copyright © Michael Kewley 1999
Second Edition 2006
Third Edition (revised) 2009

No part of this publication may be reproduced, stored in a retrieval system or transmitted, in any form or by any means, electronic, mechanical, photocopying, recording or otherwise, without prior permission of the publishers. This book is sold subject to the condition that it shall not by way of trade or otherwise, be lent, re-sold, hired out or otherwise circulated without the publishers prior consent in any form of binding cover other than that in which it is published and without similar condition including this condition being imposed on the subsequent purchaser.

ISBN 978-1-899417-03-2

Published by:
Panna Dipa Books.
e-mail:
dhammateacher@hotmail.com

DEDICATION

For my sons,
Michael & Adam

Life changing magic

> Mind can be our best friend,
> or our greatest enemy.
>
> Dhammachariya Paññadipa

Life changing magic

Note about this Second and Third Edition

When I first wrote this small book in 1999, I had only the thought to share with people the beneficial power of the mind, and how to use it.

From my many years of training in the Buddhist traditions of Theravada and Zen, I have seen my own life open like a flower, by empowering love and letting go of fear. Essentially, everything always comes to these two things, for it is only love that allows us to grow, and always fear that keeps our life small and anxious.

It seems to me that so many people feel lost in their life because they do not know how to open the door to their own liberation, to let go of their fear, empower their love, and so be happy.

This small book was my support to all those who wanted to go further and taste a 'real' life, a more productive life, a happier life.

I am happy therefore to be asked to present a second and third edition of this small book, to continue to assist others on this special journey.

In the reviewing of the contents, I have made small changes and added more illustrative stories to the second edition.

Michael Kewley
Dhammachariya Paññadipa
France,
January 2009

Life changing magic

Foreword

We are living in a time commonly known as the 'New Age'. A time when ancient philosophies are restored, and spiritual understanding revitalised.

But so much of the 'New Age', is empty and pointless. It doesn't help us understand the cause of our suffering or how to end it. Like everything else in our life it only addresses the symptoms of our unhappiness, not their origination.

Not so with Vipassana, and not so with Michael Kewley. I have known Michael as a teacher, and then friend for many years and the joy of sitting with him in a Dhamma Hall and listening to him speak stays with me.

Michael and Vipassana come straight to the point - and stays there!

Neither are concerned with fantasy or new and interesting ideas, only with ending our suffering and unhappiness in life.

Michael is a Dhamma Master of international reputation, and a wonderful story teller. Just when he has us relaxed and laughing at one of his stories, he shoots the arrow of Truth straight into our hearts.

'Would you like to live a life free from unhappiness and discontent?', he asks, 'Well, who's stopping you?' And this is the point of Vipassana.

The person responsible for your experience of life is you, and only you. The moment you realise this fundamental truth, you are free. And, if you really want your life to be different, it can be, but you must make the effort.

This is the teaching of Vipassana, and the following are

the words of Michael.

To meet and connect spiritually with a teacher can be called the greatest blessing in life, and whether this is done in person or through the pages of a book, the impact will be profound.

I wish success and happiness to all those who read these words.

Matthew Kendrick
Vipassana International

Vipassana

If we truly want to see, know and comprehend reality, we must meditate.

The meditation practice of Awareness is traditionally called Satipatthana, but in modern language we use the name Vipassana. This word does not describe a technique of meditation, but rather the purpose of that meditation - to see things as they really are.

There are many different schools, styles and forms of Vipassana practice, but in truth, anything that cultivates clear and unclouded vision of each moment can be called Vipassana.

The Buddha himself did not prescribe a certain meditation technique for the development of awareness, rather he recommended that his followers (bhikkhus) be aware in every moment and in every action, both physical and mental.

This practice, of course, should be cultivated not only in the formal sitting meditation, but in each moment of daily life.

Taken from 'The Other Shore', by Michael Kewley.
Published by Pannadipa Books.

Life changing magic

Contents

Note about Second & Third Edition

Foreword

Vipassana

Introduction

Part One
Understanding Affirmations

Part Two
Constructing Affirmations

Part Three
Writing Affirmations

Part Four
Using Affirmations

Affirmation Meditation

Postscript

Life changing magic

Introduction

I first became aware of the power of affirmation practice in 1991 in the small town of Budh Gaya, Northern India, the place where, according to tradition, Siddhartha Gotama, the Buddha, attained enlightenment.

I was conducting my annual series of ten day intensive Vipassana Retreats at the International Meditation Centre, when during a few days rest, I met with disaster. For reasons which even now cannot be logically explained, a fire occurred in my room. Although the room itself was not damaged, the fire destroyed almost all my clothes, most of my possessions and money, and left me completely devastated. My immediate reaction was to run. What else could I do? I had no money and no clothes. I felt completely lost!

Friends, of course rallied round, but all I could think of was returning to the safety of England. It was then I was introduced to the power of affirmation.

One former student of mine was also a student of Tibetan Buddhism and on the afternoon of the fire she visited me and asked if I had ever heard of affirmations. At that point I had not, and viewed what she told me with great scepticism.

The secret of affirmations had been passed to her by a Tibetan Lama she said, and had the power to transform my life, to create special conditions in my life, and was the source of real magic in the world. She then gave me numerous examples of how affirmations had helped her; from getting jobs she was not qualified for over other extremely qualified people, to relationships she wanted and even material security. I doubted it all, but

fortunately had nothing to loose!
So, having received the instruction on how to construct and use my own personal affirmation, I began.
I was truly amazed! Within days things began to change for me dramatically. Money came, people came, help came, kindness came. My life began to manifest everything I had affirmed.
It didn't take very long for me to see and experience the power and magic of affirmations, but being a Vipassana practitioner, I wanted to understand exactly how it worked.
I began to investigate this phenomena and gradually came to understand the mechanics of it. The power of affirmation practice is magical, that is true, but it is grounded in, dare I say it, common sense. It is an extremely logical system of holistic personal development.
Two years later, again in Budh Gaya and on intensive retreat in a private interview situation with a student, I felt that this person would benefit from the practice of affirmation. So, having discussed his situation in detail we wrote his own personalised affirmation. Again the results were remarkable. From someone who was shy, withdrawn and very uncomfortable in the company of others, this person transformed into an outward going, confident young man, able to walk easily through many difficult situations in his life.
I met this young man two years after this meeting to find that his development had continued, and that he had become the person he really was, and wanted to be. As a support to my own students involved in a deep practice of Vipassana and Loving Kindness meditation and living, I have often given affirmations to deepen

their transformation. Always working with them so that what they affirm is not general, but unique and personal to them. In every case the results have been the same. Deep-seated changes of personality, from the negative to the positive.

Since that time I have presented many affirmation workshops in the U.K. and Europe, helping people to understand that the power to change their lives and realise their true potential lies entirely in their own hands.

There is real magic in the world, and it lies in the power of Vipassana Affirmation.

This book is a response to the many requests that have been made to create a practical information source based upon those workshops, that will be readily available to everyone.

> May all beings benefit from this simple practice,
> May all beings realise their true potential,
> May all beings be happy.

Michael Kewley
Isle of Man
United Kingdom
December 1997

Life changing magic

Part One
Understanding Affirmations

Life changing magic

We are what we think.
All that we are arises with our thoughts,
and with our thoughts we make our world.

> Siddhartha Gotama
> (The Buddha)

Life changing magic

Understanding Affirmations

It may seem that affirmation practice is something new for you, something you have never done before and something that may, or may not, bring about the results you would like.
However, this is not really the case.
The practice of affirming is something that every human being from every social and cultural background is actively engaged in from the earliest part of their life.
Affirmations are something we all use, not only day to day, but actually, moment to moment.
Sadly, the type of affirmations we empower in our ordinary everyday life, are negative affirmations!

Negative Affirmations

Negative Affirmations are the habits we have accumulated since our childhood of continually telling ourselves that we are not very good at something, or very often, everything.

Reflect upon your own life, how many times do you negatively affirm something?

How many times do you tell yourself that you are not very good at a particular thing even before you attempt it?

How many times do you expect to fail at something before you even begin?

This is negative affirmation and it's power is phenomenal!

Before we begin a new venture we tell ourselves that we will surely fail, and when we do we're not surprised are we? Why should we be, after all, didn't we just predict it?

As human beings we are nothing more than the accumulation of the conditioning we received throughout our young lives, and the overwhelming majority of this conditioning is negative.

From our childhood we are taught to believe in one way or another, that we are simply 'not good enough'. Not only that, but no matter how hard we try, we are never going to be.

Even though this is not true, we believe it, and then continually reinforce this belief.

People from my generation were told that 'children

should be seen and not heard', and on a Sunday afternoon my sister and myself would be dressed in our best Sunday clothes and taken by our parents to their friends' house. There we would be told to sit on the settee, keep quiet, don't interrupt, and don't get dirty!

As adults we may now be able to smile at this treatment, and perhaps even treat our own children in this way, but just take a moment to reflect. What was the message that our parents were giving us.

They were telling us that we were not really good enough to take part in that aspect of life. We were being shown our place, and instructed to know it and remember it! I am quite certain that my parents loved my sister and myself as much as any parents love their children, but they too, in the end, were only the product of their own conditioning.

And this conditioning stays with us!

We rarely leave our family, social and cultural programming behind us, but carry it forward into every moment. Even when we are adults we are still just as much subject to this type of negative conditioning as we were in our childhood years.

Have you ever sat with your boyfriend or girlfriend in a beautiful, romantic setting? Perhaps a cosy room, with the lights low, a glass of wine and some soft music playing gently in the background? You look at the person opposite you, the one you love so much, and think, 'what do they see in me?'

Now, why would you ever think something like that? Why would you ever think that you are not worthy of the love and respect of another person?

Negative conditioning!

And the curious thing is that your partner is probably sitting opposite you, uncertain of themselves and wondering the same thing.
Our negative conditioning is very strong and dictates every aspect of our relationships, our work and our life in general. It colours everything we think, do and say and usually, without investigation at least, is completely invisible to us. It's just who we are!
We rarely trust our own judgement and spend so much time seeking the approval of others. Always asking, 'What do you think?'

The jacket
At one time my wife and myself were going to a rock and roll concert. I had been in town that day and bought from a charity shop, the very thing I wanted. It was a black jacket, one size too big, so that it hung from my shoulders and with sleeves so long I had to turn back the cuffs so the lining showed. This was a popular fashion at the time and I felt very happy at my discovery. I felt even happier when I put my hand in a pocket and found a badge from a famous 'seventies television rock programme, called 'The Old Grey Whistle Test', which I immediately pinned on the lapel.
Getting ready that evening I put on my best T shirt, my best jeans, my best boots and finally, the crowning glory - the new jacket.
I looked in the mirror and liked what I saw. I thought,

'Yes, Mr Cool!'.
I went downstairs to where my wife was waiting and entered the room. The moment she saw me she was horrified and exclaimed 'You're not going out like that are you?'
Immediately I was crushed. All the confidence I had felt whilst alone in the bedroom left me and I became the small child in front of his parents again. I mumbled something under my breath and went straight back upstairs to change my jacket. Something much more conventional.

We stand in front of the mirror having spent an hour getting ready to go out, and then turn to our partner and ask them what they think. Don't we know for ourselves when we look good? Why is the opinion of someone else always more important than the confidence in our own judgement?

Negative conditioning!

In the play Hamlet, by William Shakespeare there is the famous line:

> This above all, to thine own self be true.

This, I think, is very beautiful and when I reflect upon the power of this simple sentence, it feels as though my heart opens. I feel a tremendous surge of joy and a real connectedness to everything. However, the problem here lies in the fact that we don't know what our own self really is! We only know what we are from what others have told us we are, and mostly they are telling us that we are not very good.

Again reflect, if one hundred people come up to you in the street and tell you that you are a wonderful, warm, funny, caring and generous person, and then later one person tells you that you are mean, bad tempered, unkind and unpleasant, who do you believe?

The hundred or the one? And why should that one opinion outweigh the hundred others?

Negative conditioning!

It is because we are always tapping into our enormous storehouse of negative conditioning and our endless supply of unkind, and untrue views and feelings about ourselves.

When we are continually negatively affirming what we perceive to be our own shortcomings, they become our reality. The Buddha's teaching of cause and effect makes clear this point:

> We are what we think.
> All that we are arises with our thoughts,
> and with our thoughts we make our world.

So what do you think?

Or, more importantly, what do you think about yourself? It is necessary to understand this, because it is the very empowering of those thoughts that is determining your experience of the world.

Do you affirm your own positive qualities, or your negative ones?

If, as with the majority of people in the Western world, you habitually affirm your negative qualities they will continue to manifest in your life. If you tell yourself that you are not very good at something, do you think you will be? If you tell yourself a thousand times that you are not very good at it, will you become better or worse?
If you keep telling yourself that you hate your job or your life, do you think that these conditions will improve?

You decide!

Perhaps you are like the man at work who was rushing around telling everyone, 'I'm having a crisis, I'm having a crisis!' and to be sure, he was!

It is important for us to be honest and look impartially at our life.
How do we see ourselves? What and where is our position in every aspect of relationship, whether at work, at home or socially? Do we place ourselves above, below or equally with others.

Jones, Jones, Jones and Jones.
One day a man telephoned his firm of lawyers.
As soon as the telephone was answered, the man asked if he may speak to Mr Jones.
"I'm afraid Mr Jones is not here today," came the reply.
"Oh, then could I speak with Mr Jones?"
"I'm sorry," the voice answered, "Mr Jones is in court today."
"Then could I please speak to Mr Jones," continued the

man.
"Mr Jones is on holiday and will not be back until next week," was the response.
"Oh, so pehaps I could speak with Mr Jones," asked the man.
"Good morning," came the reply, "Mr Jones speaking, how may I help."

In every moment we are creating our story, but that story is always established on our past habits, our likes and dislikes and more importantly, our fears and anxieties. Each time we act on these 'old friends', we plant the seeds for the future.

Jesus said the same in the famous phrase:

As ye sow, so shall ye reap.

So what seeds are you sowing? The seeds of low self-esteem and failure, or success?
The truth is that if we prepare ourselves for failure, then we will fail. Whatever we affirm will become our reality, and there is no escape from this.
We are what we think (we are), and we reap what we sow. If we think that we are worthless and untalented, then this is how we will appear to ourselves and others because that will become our reality. If we sow the seeds of failure then that will be the outcome of what we do, simply because in our mind, we block the possibility of success. Failure becomes our reality. We empower it and so realise it.
This short story may help to illustrate this fundamental

truth.

The wish fulfilling tree

At one time a man was resting under a tree, having spent most of the day walking to his home. He was hot, tired and very hungry. As he sat there in the shade, he thought to himself, 'I wish I had something nice to eat.'

He didn't realise it but the tree he was sitting under was a wish fulfilling tree, and anything a person wished for under this tree would immediately become real, and so instantly, with this thought, a beautiful banquet table appeared, filled with the most delicious food.

The man, without thinking further ate as much as he could and returned to sit under the tree. 'Now,' he thought, 'I wish I had something good to drink,' and with that thought a huge array of drinks appeared arranged on a beautifully prepared table. The man sampled everything he could until he was not able to take another drop, even of the finest wine.

Sitting under the tree again he began to reflect that his home was still a long way in the distance. 'Oh, how I wish my home was near to me now,' he thought, and suddenly his home appeared to him just over the nearest hill. There when he looked, he could see his wife working in the yard and his children playing nearby.

He must have been quite a slow witted man because it was only now that he realised something special was happening under this tree.

'This tree must be a magic tree,' he thought, 'and if it is, I am sure it is inhabited by a huge, fierce ogre.' Just in that moment the huge ogre appeared and let out a ferocious roar.

'Oh no,' thought the man, 'now I am sure that he will eat me,' and that's exactly what the ogre did!

And the moral of this story is:

> That which we fear will be cast upon us.

We bring about the things we fear because we empower those thoughts. We make them real for ourselves, and those thoughts dictate the experience of our world.
So, what are your negative affirmations?
How well or how badly do you think of yourself? What fears do you project into your life, and so into your world?

Here are some common negative affirmations:

> I COULD NEVER DO THAT.
> I'M NO GOOD IN RELATIONSHIPS.
> PEOPLE DON'T LIKE ME.
> I NEVER HAVE ANY MONEY.
> I'M NOT ATTRACTIVE TO MEN / WOMEN.
> I'M NOT ATTRACTIVE TO MYSELF.
> I'M SHY / UNINTERESTING.
> I'M ALWAYS OVERLOOKED FOR PROMOTION.
> LIFE IS HARD.
> YOU'VE GOT TO WORRY.

In understanding affirmations we have to realise that every thought we act upon or empower has an effect. For example, if we believe that we are shy and inferior in a situation, that is exactly what we will become. These thoughts will manifest themselves in the way we hold our body, the way we use our speech and the way we relate to the situation in general.

Whatever we think we will become and the being that we become (by empowering these thoughts) will be received and interpreted by others. Again, there is no way around this. Body language is a fact! The way we sit, stand, walk and talk is only a reflection of our mind state in any moment. Whenever we empower negative affirmations or qualities of low self-esteem, that is exactly what will manifest into the world from us.

Look around at any party. Who is sitting in the corner nursing a drink, wishing they weren't there? The confident person of the timid person?

And which one are you?

Positive Affirmations

It's said that in the universe there are only two forces, the force of fear and the force of love. Fear serves only to close us down to life, while love opens us up to life and all its possibilities. Negative affirmations feed the fire of fear. Positive affirmations feed the fire of love.

For most people, the fire of fear is blazing brightly like a bonfire in November, whilst the fire of love is a small pile of barely glowing embers. Every time we affirm something negative we feed the fire of fear and it just gets bigger and bigger. We can feel trapped into a life and way of living that we don't like or enjoy, but lack any conviction or confidence to do anything about it.

We may feel that life is something just to be coped with day after day, week after week, month after month and year after year. We may even put everything down to chance. To think that we never have any real luck in our lives, whilst others always seem to have the best of it.

In every situation, we can always justify and explain our fear, and so make it acceptable.

However, if we investigate honestly, we will see that luck is not just blind chance. Luck is the ability to see the potential in every situation.

Winning the lottery

At one time St Peter was looking down from heaven at an old priest who was living a quiet and simple life. Peter was impressed by what he saw and approached God with a request.

"Lord," he said, "this old priest has led a wonderful life. I think it would be kind to let him win the lottery in his old

age."
God replied, "Peter, I can't do that."
Peter was persistent and implored God, "Please Lord, help him. He has always been a good priest and served you well."
God again replied, "Peter, I'm sorry, but I can't do that."
For the third time Peter asked God, "Lord, this priest always took care of the poor, the old and the sick. I think that it would be a kindness to let him win the lottery."
"Peter," said God, "I have told you twice already that I cannot help him."
"But why Lord, why won't you let him win the lottery?" cried Peter.
"Because he won't buy a ticket!" answered God.

If we don't invest, how can we have the possibility of winning? And now is the time to invest in ourselves.
There is a real and persistent imbalance within us, but now it is time to make the effort to change so that our life becomes joyful and invigorating, and is experienced, not as something only to be coped with, but something that is lived freely, fully and lovingly.

If our negative affirmations manifest in everything we think, do and say, so will our positive ones. This positive manifestation will be received by the people we come into contact with and they will see us differently.
We will be creating a new and vibrant world for ourselves.

When my teacher of affirmations told me that she had been selected for a job she was not qualified for, above others who were extremely qualified, I was initially sceptical. However, upon reflection, it becomes obvious as to how and why that could happen.

First she would affirm her own qualities of confidence and self worth. This would allow her to even apply for a job she was not qualified for.

Secondly, at the interview, she would manifest these qualities and they would be received by the interviewers. They would know, of course, that she did not have the required qualifications, but something in her manner would impress them, so much, in fact, that they would offer her the position.

Of course we are not talking here about brain surgery or flying an aircraft, these are skills that take many years to master, however, even in these areas positive affirmations will help us to acquire the work we really want rather than just being another name on a list.

Some positive affirmations are:

> I AM AN INTERESTING PERSON TO BE WITH.
> I LOVE LIFE.
> I AM CONFIDENT AND OUTWARD GOING.
> I AM ATTRACTIVE TO MYSELF AND OTHERS.
> I EXCEL AT WHATEVER I DO.
> I AM NOTICED BECAUSE OF MY ACHIEVEMENTS.
> I AM KIND AND COMPASSIONATE.
> I AM WORTHY OF THE LOVE AND RESPECT
> OF EVERYONE I MEET.
> I AM HAPPY IN MY LIFE.
> I AM ABLE TO RESPOND TO EVERY SITUATION.

When we affirm qualities such as these in our life, we

will find that they become our reality. When we affirm kindness and generosity in our life, we will naturally and spontaneously become kind and generous people. When we affirm happiness in our life, we will become happy people. The Buddha's teaching of cause and effect works with positive thoughts in exactly the same way it works with negative thoughts.

> We are what we think.
> All that we are arises with our thoughts,
> and with our thoughts we make our world.

Perhaps you will ask, "But where will all these wonderful positive qualities come from?"
And this is an important question, where will they come from?
Are we really creating a brand new and completely different person from thin air?
The understanding of this answer is as important as the question.

In the practice of affirming we are not creating a new and wonderful person from nothing. We are simply allowing the qualities that we already have but suppress, to manifest in our life.
Our heart needs no improvement, it only needs the freedom to express itself. There is nothing for you to get or create. You are already all the things you want to be.
With positive affirmation practice you will be able to realise this for yourself and so change the way that you experience your life. From unhappy to happy, from negative to positive, from fearful to loving.

The two camels

At one time two camels were talking, when the first one asked a question. "Excuse me for asking, but why do we have this huge hump on our back?"

"Ah," said the second camel, "this hump is very special and very important. We are ships of the desert and because of this hump we can store fat and live without food and water for many days. Oh yes, this hump is very special and very important."

"Oh I see," said the first camel, "but why do we have such long eyelashes?"

"Ah," said the second camel, "our eyelashes are very special and very important. We are ships of the desert and because of our eyelashes, no matter how much sand is blowing in the wind we can continue to walk without getting lost. Oh yes, our eyelashes are very special and very important."

"Oh I see," said the first camel, "but why do we have such big feet?"

"Ah," said the second camel, "our feet are very special and very important. We are ships of the desert and because of our feet, which expand when we walk, no matter how soft the sand is we can continue our journey without getting stuck. Oh yes, our feet are very special and very important."

"Oh I see," said the first camel, "so what are we doing in London zoo?"

When we already have everything we need to live a full, free flowing and loving life to the highest quality, why are we not doing so?

Our potential as human beings is there to be accessed,

not ignored. It is there to be used, not disregarded. By accessing these qualities that we already have in abundance, we will realise our own birthright.

A life lived to the full. A creative and productive life that can be experienced as a joy and a benefit to ourselves and others.

A life where we can truly be the person that we already are.

Or as one Zen Master once said:

> When you have a choice, choose the best!

Life changing magic

Part Two
Constructing Affirmations

Life changing magic

Be careful what you wish for.

Life changing magic

Constructing Affirmations

St Pauls Cathedral
At one time Sir Christopher Wren was visiting the site of St Pauls Cathedral.
He saw some men working and remaining incognito, he asked each in turn what they were doing.
"I'm just moving some stones," said the first.
"I'm just digging a hole," said the second.
Disapointed with this lack of enthusiasm, he aproached the third man.
"What are you doing here?" asked Sir Christopher.
"Me?" replied the man, "Why I'm helping to build a great cathedral."

Constructing a personal affirmation is a very precise science, after all, we are radically changing the very source of our own experience of life, namely the mind itself and it's manifestations. We need to know exactly what changes we want to bring about and be very sure of our intentions.
Once we begin this path we will receive exactly what we affirm.
As a male or female fantasy we may feel that it would be wonderful to be the centre of attention with the opposite sex, to have admirers constantly on our arm or calling us on the telephone at every opportunity, but as a reality the opposite is more likely to be true. Never to have a moments peace, never being able to have a quiet time alone. Being the centre of attention may not be the blessing we fantasise about, so leave fantasies aside and reflect carefully on how you would really like your life to

be.

Before continuing with this section take some time for yourself and consider:

> If you could be any way you want,
> how would you be?
> What qualities would you have
> and how would they manifest
> in different situations?

Imagine the perfect you, living and acting in the world. If you are shy, perhaps you would affirm confidence. If you are habitually angry or irritated, perhaps you would affirm peacefulness and an easy going manner. But this is your affirmation, and it is for you to decide. If you could be any way you want, how would you be?

Take your time. Think slowly and carefully and write down the qualities you think that you don't have, but would like. Make a list.
This list can be as long or as short as is necessary, but if it contains only one or two items you probably don't need affirmations. It is true that not everyone needs affirmations, but it is also true that everyone can benefit from them.
If your list has twenty items then the probability is that you have, in one way or another, duplicated some, but in making the list simply write down spontaneously whatever comes to mind. All of your perfect characteristics. Later you can review your list and erase those qualities that appear more than once.

Remember: Your perfect qualities can be anything!

One person I worked with affirmed physical beauty, another femininity, another confidence (the most common affirmation), another person affirmed a loving personality, and so the list goes on. All these affirmations were successful and in one way or another, life changing. But all these affirmations were unique and personal to the person involved. It is what they thought, not what I or someone else thought. They were the qualities that these particular people felt they lacked in their life.

Remember: What you believe to be true becomes true for you!

The psychiatrist
At one time a man visited a psychiatrist and was was given the famous 'ink blot' test, where he had to say quickly what he saw in a series of random images on individual cards.

The test began and the psychiatrist showed the first image.

"That is a man and woman making love," said the man without hesitation.

"And that?" asked the psychiatrist as he showed the second card.

"That is another man and woman making love," answered the man instantly.

"And this one?" said the psychiatrist.

"This is another man and woman making love. "

" Very good" said the psychiatrist, "I think I have your problem resolved. You are a sex maniac!"

"Me!" exclaimed the man, "You're the one with the dirty pictures."

When we look out into the world through the media or simply with our ordinary daily contact, what we really see are millions of people continually affirming that which they believe to be true.
It is here that Vipassana Affirmations really work, not by changing our belief systems, one for another, but by letting go of our negative limiting views of ourselves.

Generally, what we affirm are the opposites of what we believe to be our natural dispositions.
Some examples to help you are listed here.

A person who believes they are:

> JEALOUS.
> SHY / LACKS CONFIDENCE.
> UNINTERESTING.
> NOT GOOD WITH MONEY.
> UNCREATIVE.
> POOR COMMUNICATOR.
> UNPOPULAR.
> ANGRY / IRRITABLE.
> LAZY / LACKS ENTHUSIASM FOR LIFE.
> JUDGEMENTAL / OPINIONATED.

Would affirm their opposite values, such as:

> TRUSTING NATURE.
> CONFIDENCE.

INTERESTING.
GOOD WITH MONEY.
CREATIVE / RESOURCEFUL.
ARTICULATE.
POPULAR.
PEACEFUL.
ENERGETIC.
NON JUDGEMENTAL / FREE FROM OPINIONS.

Our list contains the virtues we believe we don't have, but would like. But once again it is important to remind you that the qualities we feel we would like to express in our lives are qualities that we already have, but simply don't access. We are not creating a brand new individual from nothing. We are only putting fuel now on the fire of love, at the expense of the fire of fear.
We are already everything we want to be, we just don't realise it yet.
And we don't have to get rid of our negative qualities either. We just stop adding fuel to them. When we affirm our positive qualities, they will grow, naturally and spontaneously. When we stop feeding our negative qualities they will die by themselves. We don't have to destroy them!

When the Buddha was asked, 'What is the best way to put out a fire?' he replied, 'Simply don't add any more fuel to it, that way it goes out by itself!'

We allow the fire of our own low self-esteem and negativity to die out by itself, by no longer feeding it, and we transfer our energy to the fire of high self-esteem and positive self view allowing it to grow and develop by energising that aspect of our being.

Our negative view of ourselves is convincing, but it's not true!

Whatever qualities we feel that we have are not set in stone. They are not fixed. They can be changed. All we have to do is raise the intention to live our life to its fullest potential, and be the person that we already are.
We do this by simply replacing our negative view of ourselves with a positive one.
This positive view then becomes our reality and so determines our experience of the world.
If our world is governed by all, or even some of the ten examples of negative qualities, what will be our experience of life? Pleasant or unpleasant?
If we change our way of being to the positive qualities, how will that affect our experience of life? Will it increase our happiness or not?
Once we understand that happiness and a sense of fulfilment is something that we can determine for ourselves, we will have grasped the power behind affirmation practice.

The frog and the scorpion
At one time a frog was relaxing in the sunshine on a lily pad in the middle of a slow running river. He was happily enjoying the gentle heat on his skin when his attention was suddenly attracted to the far bank as he heard someone calling him. As he looked across the river he was surprised to see a scorpion standing by the water's edge.

"Hey frog," said the scorpion, "please help me. I need to get across the river and I can't swim. Will you let me climb on your back and then you can carry me across?"

"You're kidding." said the frog. "If I come too close you will sting me with your tail and kill me."

"No," said the scorpion, "I won't harm you, I need to get across the river and you are my only hope. Please help me."

The frog listened for some time to the pleas of the scorpion until finally he was convinced to help. He swam to the bank and allowed the scorpion to climb on his back.

As he and his passenger reached the very middle, and deepest part of the river, the scorpion raised his tail and stung the frog.

As the frog felt the poison race through his body he looked up at the scorpion sitting on his back. "Why did you do that?" he asked, "Now you have killed us both."

"I know," said the scorpion sadly, "but I couldn't help it. It's my nature you see."

The scorpion could not change his nature and so acted accordingly, destroying the frog and himself. However, we are not condemned to a life like that. We can change our nature if we wish, and the power to change lies in our own hands.

Reflect upon yourself. Take some time. Go for a walk and think, 'If I could be any way I wanted to be, how would I be? What qualities would I have and how would I behave in different situations? What would the perfect me do? How would I look, and how would others respond to me?'

Whatever qualities spontaneously, or through reflection,

reveal themselves to you are the very qualities you need to affirm in your life.

Write a list and consider what you have written. It is important that this list is about what you feel about you, not what you think someone else feels about you. So keep it private!

When your list is finished look at it again. If it seems to be a long list, investigate how many times you have said the same thing in different ways.

If you have written (for example):

> Self Assuredness.
> Ability to put myself forward.
> Strength to be myself.
> Relaxed in the company of others.
> At ease with the opposite sex.

These can all be expressed by the one word, confident. But as you use this word in your own personal affirmation, it will express all the different aspects of your own unique list.

If you have written (for example):

> Giving.
> Sharing.
> Considerate.
> Kind.

Then these qualities can be expressed by the one word, generous.

Again, when using the word generous in your personal affirmation it will contain for you all the different aspects listed above.

However, these are only examples to help you. When you come to write your affirmation in the next section, you will see that the choice of word you use is important for you. It is what you feel to be encompassed by each particular word, not what someone else thinks, or even if it is correct English grammar. It is the feeling behind the word that is important.

One young Dutch woman wanted to affirm an easy going nature, rather than the highly reactive nature she had cultivated during her life. I suggested the word 'flowing' as in 'flowing with life' but she thought for a moment and arrived at the word 'soft'.

To me personally, the word 'soft' does not express the same thing as 'flowing', but for this young Dutch woman it expressed exactly what she felt. The choice of word we use to express the qualities and shades and tones of those qualities is unique and personal to us.

The word we choose is only ever a label for the qualities we wish to affirm, so choose your words with care.

Life changing magic

Part Three
Writing Affirmations

Life changing magic

Even if we could train a parrot
to recite a Vipassana Affirmation,
it's life would not change at all.

Life changing magic

Writing Affirmations

Taking care
At one time a young man ordained as a monk in a traditional Christian order.
He had been an academic student and was naturally interested in the process of copying the ancient teachings.
The abbot told him that as there was only one copy of the original manuscript the monks had to be very careful and so this original edition was locked away in a special cupboard and never taken or removed from the library. As the manuscript was so precious and delicate, all the copies now used as guides and references for the highest instructions and teachings, were taken only from the original copies that were first made - never the master!
The young monk asked if he could look at the original version, and after some persuasion the abbot permitted it.
He was accompanied by a senior monk to the library who supervised the viewing. The young monk gently and with great care began to examine this special and precious book. Suddenly something caught his eye and he pointed it out to the senoir monk.
The senior monk looked for a moment, let out a scream and ran in shock through the monastery. The abbot stopped him and asked the reason for the behaviour.
The senior monk looked at him with wide eyes and cried, "It's celebrate, the word is celebrate, not celibate!"

Having taken enough time to carefully consider which qualities we want to affirm in our life, it is now time to write them properly. Again, this part of the process is

important, so take time and care with it. Find a quiet place at a time when you won't be easily disturbed and begin.
You will need some paper and a pen. Make an effort and use a good quality paper and a pen that writes well. The writing of this life changing affirmation is an important moment, so make it a quality moment also. Have your list in front of you. Relax and begin.

How will you start?

The writing of an affirmation is like writing a letter to the person you love most in the world. Actually, when we truly understand this process we will see that this is exactly the nature of affirmations. A love letter to yourself, and so the language that we use must be the language of love.
Gentle, yet powerful!
Each word on your list has to be empowered with meaning and include all the different nuances that your chosen word reveals to you.
Even if we could train a parrot to recite a Vipassana Affirmation, it's life would not change at all. The power of affirmation lies in the personal understanding of the word, and not the word itself. So, for one more time, reflect: What do the words on your list mean to you? How will the inclusion of these qualities into your life change your experience of it?

Here then, are two example affirmations.
In each example the first list represents a personal self view cultivated over many years of negative affirming,

whilst the second list is the qualities to be affirmed.

Example One:

Negative qualities.
- Shy / Lacks confidence.
- Clumsy / inelegant.
- Cold / unfeeling.
- Lacking clear direction in life.
- Selfish.
- Low self-esteem.
- Unpopular.
- Unattractive.

Positive qualities.
- Confident.
- Graceful.
- Having clear direction in life.
- Caring and generous.
- Worthy.
- Popular.
- Attractive to others.

Example Two:

Negative qualities.
- Jealous / insecurity.
- Deceitful / manipulative.
- Lazy.
- Miserable.
- Fearful / anxious.
- Grasping.

Dishonest.
Needing money.

Positive qualities.
- Trusting.
- Honest.
- Energetic / enthusiastic.
- Happy / joyful.
- Calm / peaceful.
- Sharing.
- Truthful.
- Financial needs easily met.

With our list of positive qualities based upon the contrast with our negative self view, we can begin to write our affirmation.

The beginning of our personal affirmation is extremely important. We are not wishing for these qualities to appear in our lives as if by magic, we are affirming qualities that we already have, but repress.
Our affirmation therefore will not begin with a phrase like, 'I wish I was ...' but with the empowering reminder that 'I am already...'
These are the qualities that you have but don't access. The perfect you, expressed in the qualities you will affirm, is lying deep down inside you. Like a beautiful slumbering giant. It is now time to awaken that giant. Not by wishing he was awake, but rather, by gently shaking him to make certain he wakes up.

The final phrases in your personal affirmation are also

extremely important.

Our usual view of ourselves is negative. This is due only to our social and cultural conditioning. It is not a fact of who or what we are. It is only a belief system that we empowered because we didn't know any better. It's not our fault, but it is how things are.

How many times in your childhood were you told that 'You don't deserve this!' You are given a gift whilst at the same time being told that you don't deserve it, and so we grow into adulthood believing that we are undeserving people. When pleasant things happen to us, because of this conditioning, we may even ask ourselves, 'What did I do to deserve this?'

The truth is that we don't have to have done anything special in our life to deserve kindness and respect from others. It is already what we deserve, because it is our birthright.

Everyone of us deserves, always, the love and respect of others.

So the penultimate phrase of your personal affirmation will read, 'This is what I deserve.'

You do deserve a life that is happy, peaceful, financially rewarding and fulfilling.

When you understand the power of this phrase you will have begun to erode the lies that society fed you, that you were not quite good enough - ever, and so undeserving of the good things in life.

The final phrase of your affirmation is taken from the Vipassana practice of Love and will read, 'May I be well and happy.'

Self love is a primary requirement of spiritual growth, often called in modern terms Holistic Personal Development.

If you are not able to love yourself, how will you be able to love others? If you are not able to love yourself, how will you be able to allow others to love you?

We cultivate the loving heart and so actively wish the best for ourselves, to be well and to celebrate a good, long and fortunate life.

When we are happy we will share that happiness with everyone. We will smile, greet people in the street and share our pleasant feelings with the world.
When we are unhappy we feel bad and so we share those feelings with the world. We will not smile or greet people and in one way or another, we will always be looking for a fight!
So, find happiness for yourself so that everyone around you will benefit.

So, the two examples given earlier would read.

Example One:

> I am already a confident, loving and graceful person.
> I am caring and generous and have clear direction in my life.
> I am popular and attractive to others and worthy of the love and respect of everyone I meet.
> This is what I deserve, may I be well and happy.

Example Two:

> I am already a trusting, secure and truthful person.
> I have vitality and energy in my life and money comes to me easily.
> I experience happiness and joy at all times and am honest with myself and others.
> I delight in sharing my good fortune and fear has no place in my heart.
> This is what I deserve, may I be well and happy.

Reflect upon these two examples and write your own affirmation. Use language that is beautiful to you. When you have your first draught, read it through and empower the words. How does it feel?

The affirmation should energise and brighten the mind. It should have the effect of lifting the heart.

If it doesn't have this effect, change it! Take your time and make it perfect for you.

And don't hold back!

You can affirm anything you feel is missing from your life. The only rule for affirmation practice is simple:

Be careful what you wish for!

Some affirmations that have brought good and successful results for students of mine are:

PHYSICAL BEAUTY.
FINANCIAL SECURITY.
WORK OPPORTUNITIES.
ROMANCE.

FEMININITY.
GOOD HEALTH.
GREATER CREATIVITY.
ENHANCED SEXUAL RELATIONSHIP.

Part Four
Using Affirmations

Life changing magic

The world we experience,
is the one that we create for ourselves,
moment after moment.

Life changing magic

Using Affirmations

American tourist
An American tourist was standing in the grounds of an English stately home admiring the beautiful lawn. Just in that moment he was met by the lord and master of the house who politely asked him what he thought.
"Gee, the lawn is so beautiful, how do you get it to be so flat?" the tourist said.
"Oh, it's very simple really," replied he lord, "we just roll it every day with a very heavy lawn roller."
"That's great," said the tourist, "and how long do you do that for?"
"Three hundred years." replied the lord.

Having written our affirmation it is now time to introduce it into our lives as a living practice. The simple rule is 'more is better', and so the more often you use it, the greater the result will be. As with everything in our life, the effort we make determines the result we receive. However, we also have to be disciplined in our approach.

We need to commit our affirmation to memory:
Read it over and over empowering each word as you say it. Build the energy of positive thinking into your mind, and allow it to transform your experience of life. Say your affirmation slowly and meaningfully. Don't try to remember it, but let it come to you through simple repetition. Once it is clear in your memory, it will be with you in every moment and you will be able to use it as appropriate.

Always recite your affirmation in groups of seven.
If you say it once, it will always be more beneficial to say it six more times. Don't be lazy. To change a habit takes a long time, so make the effort.

There is nothing mystical about this. Seven times simply allows the energy to build and you will notice this yourself as you begin to apply the practice.

Whenever I have given affirmation practice to students sitting on Vipassana meditation retreats, I have often noticed the change in them when they do their practice in one of the formal meditation sessions. Their posture will slowly but spontaneously alter until they are sitting beautifully erect. At the end of the meditation period they will leave the Dhamma Hall walking tall with an air of confidence. Seven repetitions allows this transformation to take place.

The affirmation does not have to be spoken aloud.
If you prefer, you can do it, but it is not essential or necessary. It is only a preference.

One way of speaking your affirmation aloud is to do it in front of a mirror. Look at your own reflection as though it was someone else and speak to the image you see with love and commitment. Otherwise, when you are by yourself you can recite your affirmation aloud.

There is no special posture or place for your affirmation.
If you have a meditation practice you can include your affirmations in your daily sitting, (reciting seven times of course) silently to yourself.

You can use your affirmation when alone in the house, or even whist walking to a friend's house or to the shops.

The affirmation is yours to use wherever and whenever the opportunity arises.

The more you affirm, the greater the change.
The more often you use it on a daily basis, the more quickly the results will be experienced in your life.
However, we have to be patient but determined. Our negative conditioning is very strong and to think that by affirming once or twice every now and then will change our life radically, is unrealistic. We have to be consistent and cultivate a regular practice, using our affirmations daily. Often, when we just don't feel like it! However, these may be the very times when we will benefit most from our affirmations.
We also have to give ourselves at least one month of consistent practice before we can seriously expect to see any definite changes in our life. After that we can continue to use our affirmations to enhance and empower further those aspects of our practice that are already changing.

Revamp and revitalise your affirmations.
Once you are happy with your personal affirmation, use it as often as possible. After four or five weeks of use however, take some time to reflect and see where your life is right now. Some things will already be moving closer to you, whilst others may still seem to be only dreams on the horizon, so now is the time to look at, and possibly restructure, your affirmation. Change the expressions you have used and refine what you want. This is a building process so we need to be patient and resourceful.
If you applied for a business start-up loan from the bank

and told the manager that you would give this new venture three months to succeed or fail, it is unlikely that a loan would be approved. It takes at least twelve months (and more likely, three years) for a new business to get off the ground.

The same conditions apply to your affirmation practice. If you recite your affirmation twice a day for a year, that is still only seven hundred and thirty times. How many more times in your life have you negatively affirmed?

So, be patient, but be resolute. Refine your aims and goals and bring the things you really want closer and closer.

We can empower our affirmations even more.

To strengthen our affirmation we can write a copy and place it somewhere special. Perhaps a vase that has sentimental value, or behind a favourite photograph.

As always, there is nothing magical about this, it is simply a reminder. When we go about our daily household activities and catch sight of this special object it will remind us of our affirmation and raise the feeling in the heart. We will remember to practice, and feel the joy of what we are doing as we connect the two things together.

We can add to, or change our affirmations as we feel necessary.

Once a particular aspect of our personality has become established within us, or we feel fulfilled in our predetermined area, we can drop or change that part of the affirmation and replace it with another that now seems relevant.

Affirmations are for life, as long as we feel the need to develop.

At the beginning of our affirmation practice we need to develop trust.
We don't need to believe in affirmations, but we do need to trust the process. There are no instant remedies for anything in life, so patience will always be a requirement for everything we do. Affirmation practice is the same. No quick fix into happiness, only the trusting of a process that is grounded in truth, common sense and reality.

The world that we experience is the one that we create for ourselves moment after moment by identifying with our thoughts. If we continually identify with negative thoughts and experiences, then our world view will be negative. When we identify with positive thoughts and experiences our world view will be positive.

The world is always the world but how we see it is always unique and personal to us.

Sometimes at the beginning of affirmation practice you may find there is a little voice in your head speaking to you. Perhaps you will be affirming that you are already a kind and generous person, when this little voice will interrupt by saying, 'No you're not, you're mean and selfish!'

This little voice represents your past, your habitual way of thinking about yourself. Actually, it's not even your voice. It is the voice of your parents, your teachers, your society and most definitely needs to be ignored. Do not engage this voice in any way!

Don't speak to it or with it. Don't try to explain what you are doing to it. Don't try to make it go away. Simply ignore it and continue with your affirmation. It will soon grow tired, and once it realises that you are not listening it will have no power to return.

The past is our biggest enemy.

We carry our negative conditioning and low self-esteem with us in every moment and we are never free from it. The more we feed our perceived inadequacies, the more they become established as who and what we think we are.

We need to leave the past where it belongs - in the past!

Muddy road

At one time two monks were travelling together along a wet and muddy road. Rounding a bend they met a beautiful young women in a silk kimono and sash, unable to cross the intersection.

One monk recognised her need and immediately swept her up in his arms and carried her over the mud. The other monk followed silently and did not speak for the rest of the day. Finally they reached the monastery where they would stay for the night, but this monk could no longer restrain himself.

"We monks," he cried, "are not even supposed to look at young and beautiful women, but you actually picked one up and carried her. Why did you do that?"

"I left that young woman standing by the side of the road," said the first monk, "do you still carry her?"

This is our opportunity with affirmation practice. To let go of the past, and put down all the things we carry. To face the future, open, radiant, confident and fearless.

Everything we want is ready and waiting for us to collect.

Now we have the means to live the life we deserve. It requires only a little patience, a little determination and skilful effort.
That skilful effort is our affirmation practice.

>I wish you everything you wish for yourself.
>Be happy.

Life changing magic

Affirmation Meditation

It has already been said that it is not necessary to adopt a particular posture or method for your affirmation practice, but for those people who truly want to get the best from it, affirmation meditation is a technique to consider applying once or twice a day.

Arrange a time when you will be alone and undisturbed (i.e. away from the telephone and household responsibilities). Sit in a comfortable chair and keep your back erect, but not tense and don't allow your head to hang forward - this is the position of sleep!

Place your hands loosely in your lap and let your eyes close naturally. Let your breathing be natural also. Don't try to control or regulate it, but just allow the breath to enter and leave the body through the nose. Now, place your relaxed attention at the nostrils and see if you can experience the subtle movements of air as the body breathes.

When you feel relaxed (two or three minutes later) take your attention to the crown of the head. What can you feel?

If you are aware of something (a tingling sensation, or a slight pressure, or heat for example) just notice that. Don't be involved with it, but simply notice that you feel something. If you feel nothing just notice that you feel nothing.

Both are correct and you are not trying to make something happen, you are just noticing whatever is there.

Now, let your awareness move lightly through the whole body, relaxing each part as you come to it, and just continuing to notice any sensations or feelings that may arise.

Take your attention through the head and face, the neck, shoulders, arms and hands, chest and back, buttocks, legs and feet, finally returning to the breath in the nostrils again.

Relax but stay alert. Do not fall asleep. Keep the mind bright.

Now you can begin your affirmation. Empower each word as you mentally recite it and feel the subtle changes in the body. If you feel the desire to straighten your posture as the affirmation power begins to move into the body, do it and be aware you are responding to the suggestions.

Recite your affirmation seven times (you can keep count on your fingers) and finish with Loving Kindness. Before you open your eyes simply repeat three or four times, 'May I be well and happy. May all beings be well and happy.' Then allow your eyes to open.

Before you move, notice how you feel. Take a moment to reflect, and then continue with your day. If you practice like this, once or twice a day, you can expect the best results.

Depending on the length of your affirmation this whole simple process should take only between ten and fifteen minutes.

Useful Suggestions

Doctors advice
A man went to the doctor for a check up.
When the doctor had finished his examination he said to the man, "The best thing for you is to give up women, cigarettes and alchohol."
The man replied, "Really, what's the next best thing?"

You can affirm anything in your life, no matter how unrealistic it may appear to be on the surface. Choose what you want and affirm your first choice. Very often we feel afraid or unworthy to empower the best for us. Don't be afraid, just be careful. Is this what you really want?

Below are some suggestions for phrases you may find useful. Use them or adapt them for yourself.

I am already…..

- A HIGHLY SUCCESSFUL BUSINESSMAN / WOMAN
- A BEAUTIFUL RADIANT BEING
- A SOPHISTICATED ELEGANT WOMAN / MAN
- CREATIVE AND ARTISTIC
- OPEN AND EXPRESSIVE
- FINANCIALLY SUCCESSFUL
- HELD IN THE HIGHEST REGARD BY ALL WHO KNOW ME
- KIND AND CONSIDERATE
- LOVING
- DYNAMIC
- ARTICULATE

Calm and peaceful
Resolute and determined
A complete and perfect person
The best at what I do
Interesting and amusing
Open to all possibilities
A wonderful lover
Caring and trusting
Everything I need

I already have…..

Everything I want
Clear aims and goals in life
Success at work
Success in all my relationships
More money than I need
Many friends and the respect of all
Excellent health
An attractive and appealing body
A beautiful and interesting life
Strength and fortitude in difficult times
Personal power in my life
The ability to say 'no' to others
The ability to say 'yes' to myself
No fears in my life
Happiness and joy.

Postscript

Being lost
At one time a man went on a business trip. He decided not to fly or travel by train, but to drive himself and take the small back roads. However, after only a few hours of travelling he realised that he was completely lost. Driving down a small country road he saw a farmer sitting on the gate of a field and stopped to ask directions.
"Excuse me," he said, "do you know how far it is to London?"
"Nope," said the farmer.
"Then can you tell me how far I have come since Aberdeen?"
"Nope," said the farmer.
"Well can you tell me how to get to the motorway?"
"Nope," said the farmer.
These unhelpful answers irritated the businessman until he finally shouted at the farmer,
"You don't know very much, do you?"
"Nope," said the farmer, "but I'm not lost!"

For many people life can seem to be a difficult and complicated affair, with so many dreams dashed, so many hopes unrealised. We seem to know so many things about so many things, but not how to be happy. We feel lost.

Lost in our own life.

But with the clarity of a focused and bright mind we can realise everything we want for ourselves. Vipassana

Affirmations are not magic. They require effort and consistency of practice. If you apply yourself you can have everything. Just be sure this is what you really want.

> I wish you success and good fortune.
> May you be well and happy.

Michael Kewley
Dhammachariya Paññadipa

Life changing magic

Life changing magic

About the author

Michael Kewley is the former Buddhist monk, Paññadipa, and now an internationally acclaimed Master of Dhamma, presenting courses and meditation retreats throughout the world.

A disciple of the late Sayadaw Rewata Dhamma, he teaches solely on the instruction of his own Master, to share the Dhamma, in the spirit of the Buddha, so that all beings might benefit.

Full biography of Michael Kewley can be found at:
www.puredhamma.org

Also by Michael Kewley.
Published by
Pannadipa Books

OPENING THE SPIRITUAL HEART
HIGHER THAN HAPPINESS
NOT THIS
LIFE IS NOT PERSONAL
WALKING THE PATH
THE OTHER SHORE
THE REALITY OF KAMMA
LIFE IS NOT PERSONAL

Life changing magic

www.ingramcontent.com/pod-product-compliance
Ingram Content Group UK Ltd.
Pitfield, Milton Keynes, MK11 3LW, UK
UKHW021257180426
11947UKWH00015B/888